THE PALEOLITHIC REVOLUTION

THE FIRST HUMANS AND EARLY CIVILIZATIONS

EARLY CIVILIZATIONS

THE PALEOLITHIC REVOLUTION

Paula Johanson

For Amy Groesbeck, who showed me ancient clam gardens,
and Arianna, who is teaching me to talk and listen·

Published in 2017 by The Rosen Publishing Group, Inc.
29 East 21st Street, New York, NY 10010

Library of Congress Cataloging-in-Publication Data

Names: Johanson, Paula.
Title: The paleolithic revolution / Paula Johanson.
Description: First edition. | New York : Rosen Publishing, 2017. | Series:
  The first humans and early civilizations | Includes bibliographical
  references and index.
Identifiers: LCCN 2015050309| ISBN 9781499463163 (library bound) | ISBN
  9781499463149 (pbk.) | ISBN 9781499463156 (6-pack)
Subjects: LCSH: Paleolithic period—Juvenile literature. | Human
  evolution—Juvenile literature.
Classification: LCC GN771 .J65 2017 | DDC 930.1/2—dc23
LC record available at http://lccn.loc.gov/2015050309

Manufactured in China

CONTENTS

INTRODUCTION...6

CHAPTER 1
BONES...9

CHAPTER 2
STONES...19

CHAPTER 3
ARTIFACTS...27

CHAPTER 4
WORDS...37

CHAPTER 5
ART...42

TIMELINE...54

GLOSSARY...55

FOR MORE INFORMATION...56

FOR FURTHER READING...59

BIBLIOGRAPHY...60

INDEX...62

INTRODUCTION

To introduce the Paleolithic Revolution, it's important to talk about human origins. Scientists have compared human genes with those of great apes. They confirm our ancestors were related to the ancestors of apes long ago. The human family tree branched off from the common ancestors of humans and great apes between thirteen and seven million years ago. These hominins were species related to humans. They walked on two legs. Their descendants began using their hands, picking up rocks to bash or hack apart things for food. Their brains got bigger.

Eras of human development are named for tools made by people long ago. During the Stone Age, stones were used as tools. When people learned how to smelt metal, that began the Bronze Age and later the Iron Age. The Stone Age is considered in three distinct eras called the Paleolithic, Mesolithic, and Neolithic periods.

The Paleolithic began about 2.5 to 2 million years ago. The earliest use of tools made of stone chipped on purpose was during the Lower Paleolithic. The Middle Paleolithic was from about 200,000 years ago until 40,000 years ago. Tools made during this era showed improved flaking techniques. The Upper Paleolithic is dated between about 40,000 to 10,000 years ago in Europe and the Middle East. Those dates vary in other parts of the world. There

The people of the Paleolithic period made fine art and useful tools which show our modern scientists much about their daily lives.

were many distinct local styles of tool making during this period.

The Paleolithic Revolution got its name because anthropologists noticed a profound change in the tools made about 40,000 years ago in Europe. It looked as though people began making a much wider variety of carefully flaked stone tools. Tools were not only in stone but also in bone, ivory, and wood. Some tools had two or more parts in different materials. Some were decorated, not just with rough scratches but fine carving and stains. Carvings, engravings, and paintings on stone showed a love for fine art. Had human intelligence made a great leap forward? There were even signs that fluent speech might date to this time.

Theories about these revolutionary changes are still being adapted. Were all these changes at the same time? Or did the first change drive the others? Were these changes in one place or several?

Sites where humans used to live are more studied in Europe and the Middle East than elsewhere in the world. As other sites are being studied, new questions are asked. Did the Paleolithic Revolution happen as modern humans came to Europe? Perhaps they brought these changes with them as they traveled through western Asia into Europe. Perhaps these changes happened in Africa before modern humans journeyed to other parts of the world. Answers would be hard to prove.

These changes may have been sudden or gradual, in several places along the human journey. It is certainly fair to call this transition the Paleolithic Revolution. In the Upper Paleolithic, people had much more useful tools than in the Lower and Middle Paleolithic. There were homes, clothing, and comforts for these people. They were healthy and active. They left not only well-made tools but great art in their sculptures and paintings. They even made musical instruments of ivory and bone. Their art suggests stories were being told about their lives and the world. Their tools took great care and instruction to make. These were people who spoke fluently as they taught each other.

CHAPTER 1
BONES

Much of what we know about the Paleolithic we learned by studying the fossilized bones of our distant ancestors. The genus, or group of species, humans are in is called *Homo*. It began more than two million years ago with the species *Homo habilis* (meaning "handy man"). A later species, *Homo erectus*, stood up straight and ate a wide variety of foods. These early humans migrated throughout Africa, Europe, and Asia. There is evidence for wide variation (slim or sturdy, big teeth or small) among members of the evolving family tree of early *Homo* through several branches and

This image shows an artist's idea of what the people of the Paleolithic period may have looked like.

within small groups. *Homo heidelbergensis* was probably an ancestor for the modern human species *Homo sapiens*, which appeared about 200,000 years ago.

During the Upper Paleolithic era, there were at least four kinds of humans living. These included *Homo floresiensis* (or Flores Man), Neanderthals, Denisovans, and modern humans (our species, *Homo sapiens*).

MODERN HUMANS

As modern humans journeyed from Africa to the rest of the world, they didn't leave a record of the routes they took. But their routes and the timing of their travels can be guessed by testing DNA in mitochondria and Y chromosomes of people around the world.

Anatomically, modern humans had bones the same shape and size as humans living today. They originated in Africa and had been around for over 50,000 years when they arrived in Europe. Those living in Europe have also been called Cro-Magnons after a site in France where their bones were found. These people were tall compared to other early kinds of human. They were even taller than the average today. Men stood between 5 feet, 9 inches and 6 feet, 6 inches (175 centimeters–2 meters) with long arms and legs. Women were tall, though smaller and slighter than the tallest men. Different heights and sizes for men and women usually means they have different activities from childhood

GENETIC STUDY

Inside the cells of every living creature are chromosomes containing DNA. This long molecule carries directions for cell function. People inherit half of their DNA from their mother and half from their father. The mother's egg cell also carries mitochondria, with separate tiny packets of DNA that do not combine. Children inherit exactly the same mitochondrial DNA that their mother had and her mother had. Once in a long while, a mutation causes a small change in that DNA. Those mutations happen at a fairly steady rate, like a clock ticking slowly.

Scientists compare these mutations to create a family tree for the human race. Everyone alive today is descended from a woman who lived in Africa less than 200,000 years ago. The journey of her descendants can be followed from Africa into Asia and from Asia to Europe, Australia, and the Americas.

The Y chromosome in men changes only by mutation. These mutations can be compared and show humans spreading out along similar routes. Some estimates suggest the first modern humans left Africa around 125,000 years ago. Other estimates suggest another journey associated with distinctive stone tools occurring around 60,000 years ago. Genetic data is compared with fossils and stone tools for greater understanding.

through adulthood.

Unlike earlier kinds of humans, the faces of these people would look fairly ordinary to people today. They had high foreheads, square eye sockets with little or no browridge, and prominent chins. Their brains were a little larger than the average of today. Based on evidence from carvings and gene

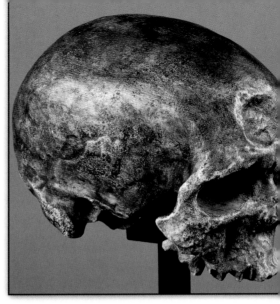

This skull was found in Abri de Cro-Magnon, the French site that gave us the name "Cro-Magnon."

analysis, these modern humans had straight hair and brown skin. If a human born during the Paleolithic Revolution could be given today's clothing and haircut, that person could walk around a big city today without looking out of place.

EFFECT OF ACTIVITIES ON BONES

Bones are a lasting record of our lives. During the Paleolithic Revolution, modern humans were strong people. Their bones had much larger muscle attachments than is common today, even for professional athletes. Their bones were harder, too. Bones from people born today are on average 15 percent weaker than bones from people born during the Upper Paleolithic era. This is due to two factors. People today are less physically active and use more kinds of tools. Physical strength is less important for survival. People then spent a lot of time walking, gathering food, and hunting. Leading active lives and using simple tools made their muscles and bones strong, just as it does for athletes and construction workers today.

Paleolithic humans used their bodies as tools, putting stress and strain on their bones and joints. As people aged, their joints and backs wore out and became damaged. Bones broke from falls or fights, causing injuries like a rodeo rider would have today. Some breaks healed well, showing signs of good care. People broke their toes because their shoes were simple wraps or soft like moccasins, not rigid-soled boots. Their feet and toes were shaped from wearing sandals or soft skin shoes, instead of splaying wide from going barefoot all the time.

Paleolithic people's lives affected their teeth, too. From chewing tough food, their jaws grew

Archaeologists can learn a lot by studying old bones, such as this Cro-Magnon skeleton from Liguria, Italy.

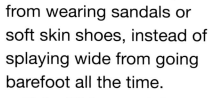

a little bigger than people today, who eat softer food. Bigger jaws meant fewer impacted wisdom teeth than today. Their teeth had fewer cavities than today, too, because they ate fewer grains and other food that sticks to the teeth. But they had other tooth problems instead. Since people used their teeth as pliers and clamps, their teeth got worn down, chipped, and even cracked. People also chewed leather to make it soft. Some old people had teeth worn down to nubs.

Injuries led to disability and shorter lives, as happens in Third World countries today. Even so, some people lived for decades with a partially disabling injury. About half the people died by age twenty. Babies were far more likely to die than is common today in developed countries. A child who survived to age five was likely to live to adulthood. There were many dangers when gathering food or hunting. However, many diseases would not become common until thousands of years later, when animals were widely domesticated. If a young woman survived giving birth, or a young man was not killed in a fight, he or she might live to be forty or fifty years old. It was rare for someone to live beyond age sixty.

OTHER RECENT HOMININS

The other kinds of humans that were alive during the Paleolithic Revolution looked different from people today. The best studied of these people are the Neanderthals, named for a German valley where their bones were found. These people had even stronger and heavier bones than the *Homo sapiens* of the Paleolithic. They were up to 5 feet, 7 inches (1.7 m) tall and had shorter arms and legs than people today. Their faces had prominent browridges and receding chins. Their brains were a little larger than the average for people today. The last Neanderthal fossils are from around 30,000 years ago.

Neanderthals are not the only other kind of human who survived until Paleolithic times. In 2003, fossil bones were found on the island of Flores in Indonesia. These people were *Homo floresiensis*, commonly called Flores Man. Informally, they are also called "hobbits," as they stood about 3.5 feet (1.1 m) tall, like the little people in books by J. R. R. Tolkien. They had small heads with receding chins, wrist bones like gorillas, teeth like *Homo erectus*, and long feet. Their most recent fossils are some 12,000 years old. However, there have been rumors on Flores, recorded since the sixteenth century, that hiding in the jungles were little, hairy people called the *ebu gogo*.

Fossil bones of another kind of human were discovered in Denisova Cave in the Altai Mountains of Siberia. DNA from a finger bone of a young girl and from two molars of large men suggest they they were distinct from modern humans and Neanderthals. They shared a common ancestor with us, perhaps *Homo heidelbergensis*, hundreds of thousands of years ago. These people are called Denisovans (their scientific name is still under debate). As for how they looked, scientists can only guess based on these few samples. The robust finger bone and big teeth suggest that Denisovans were big and very sturdy.

EFFECT OF VARIED DIET ON BONES

At the time of the Paleolithic Revolution, there was not organized farming. That skill developed much later in Neolithic times. As hunters and gatherers, people managed and maintained available food resources, both animals and plants.

Modern humans ate a range of foods that varied with the seasons and the changing climate. These varied foods supplied the vitamins, minerals, and fats necessary to grow healthy bodies and brains. Plants they harvested changed with the seasons. At the sites where these people spent time are the bones of the animals they ate. Among these animals are rabbits, horses, deer, ibex, and birds. There were aurochs, a wild version of modern cattle. In many places across Europe and western Asia, reindeer were the most commonly hunted animal. People caught fish in rivers and by the sea, using hooks and spears. Other seafood was harvested, too. Clam gardens were built along the North American Pacific coast.

Analysis of the minerals in their bones confirms these people ate cooked food. Cooking food allows more calories and nutrition to be used than raw food.

Art from the Upper Paleolithic, like this painting in Lascaux cave in France, shows animals people hunted for food. Some paintings have marks that look like arrows and spears.

Their bone minerals confirm that most people during the Upper Paleolithic spent all their lives fairly close to the area where they were born. A few people travelled far from the places where they lived as children, walking many hundreds of miles.

INTERBREEDING AMONG HUMAN SPECIES

Geneticists at Harvard University, in Massachusetts, studied the genes of present-day people and samples from Neanderthal bones. They discovered that modern humans bred with Neanderthals. Most likely this happened between 47,000 and 65,000 years ago, when modern humans were expanding their territory out of Africa.

Modern humans with roots outside of Africa have inherited some genes from other recent humans. Scientists found that people of Asian and European ancestry have about 2 to 4 percent Neanderthal DNA, while roughly 5 percent of the genes in Aboriginal Australians and Melanesians come from Denisovans. Scientists are still studying the contributions of other *Homo* species to the genetic makeup of modern humans, as well as the impact that these genes have on people today.

Chapter 2
Stones

Studying stone tools from the Upper Paleolithic era makes it easier to understand the abilities of these people, as well as what their daily lives must have been like. Scientists recognize stone that has been shaped into tools not only by its shape but also by wear marks from pounding, polishing, or cutting.

Among the first human tools were stones in Africa's Oldowan valley. A pebble can fit nicely in a person's hand. It can be thrown or used as a hammer. A broken rock with a sharp edge can be used as a hand axe to chop apart a vegetable or a dead animal. It's hard to tell when hominins began making stone tools instead of picking up any handy rock. Whack a pebble with another rock, and it can break with a sharp edge. At least one thing is clear from the tools and fossils that have been found: big brains weren't needed for simple stone tools. Our ancient ancestors used the Oldowan toolkit of hammerstone, hand axe, and broken flakes for scrapers for over a million years.

Better Stone Tools

One of the clearest ways to define the Paleolithic Revolution is that people began making much better tools. These weren't just any rock with one lucky

Experts shared techniques to make stone tools with sharp edges and exactly the right shapes needed for a complete toolkit for daily living.

break. These tools were carefully made of flint or obsidian, a stone that breaks sharp like glass. The makers learned how to strike the stones carefully to break off flakes. This skill is called knapping.

Flint knappers could use a hammerstone to chip a few flakes off a flint bigger than their fists. The core could make a basic hand axe and a few scrapers. A knapper learned to prepare the flint with a flat top for a striking platform. Then the knapper would knock away flakes around all sides of the flint. When the knapper hit the top, a big flake with sharp edges would come off. This style of flint knapping makes Levallois tools, named for a place in France where several of these tools were found.

Later knappers improved this style. Instead of hammering the flint, they would hit a piece of antler braced at the top of the flint. It was a gentle hit that would knock precise flakes away. A good knapper

QUARRIES

Knowing where to find good stone for tools was vital to survival in Paleolithic times. Since any tool could become broken, dull, or lost, a person would need more than one sharp tool. Quarries have been found where people dug and gathered flint or obsidian.

Flint quarries have been found in chalky hills. It was worth the work to dig out chunks of flint from the soft chalk. Flint that has been out in the weather for years might have cracks. It doesn't flake as well as a newly dug up piece. The best flint would be traded for hundreds of miles. Control of the mines would have been valuable. Obsidian was found near old volcanoes. It was traded in chunks and as tools over long distances, too.

could go round and round the core of a flint and strike off many flakes. Some of these flakes were retouched by pressing on the edge with a stone, bone, or antler tool. That's called pressure flaking.

TOOLS MADE FROM FLAKES

Flakes were sometimes useful just as they were formed. Often, knappers reshaped flakes. They would dull one side to make knife blades a person could hold. The base of a blade could be chipped to make it fit into a handle. Blades are generally twice as long, or longer, than they are wide. Blades are larger than bladelets, which have a width of up to about .5 inch (12 millimeters).

Microliths are tiny blades. They can be less than a third of an inch (8 mm) wide. They're too small to hold well with fingers. Microliths were made to be hafted, or set in a handle of wood, antler, or bone. In Europe and western Asia, microliths were retouched. This means their shapes were refined by flaking off more stone. In China most microblades were not retouched.

Sometimes, the shape of a flake made it natural to use for a particular kind of tool, like projectile points for spears and darts. Awls had sharp points but were strong. Burins had sharp sides with a square end. Chisels were stronger, with sides made dull and a sharp end for cutting.

NAMING TOOL TRADITIONS

Details of stone tools changed over time and in various places. Scientists name each distinct style of stone tools for the first place where they are found and dated. These subtle but distinct styles of stone tools are used to date newly found sites.

Aurignacian tools are dated about 38,000 to 32,000 years ago. These tools were strikingly different from

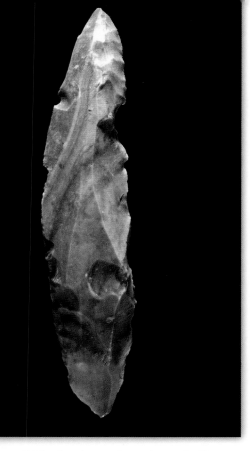

This Aurignacian stone knife was carefully shaped from flint, chipped by hard use, and resharpened by flaking.

Middle Paleolithic tools. Knappers would strike a prepared flint core carefully. Multiple small blades could be flaked off a prismatic core. A flake made into a burin could be used to score bone or ivory to make needles.

Châtelperronian tools (from about 41,000 to 33,000 years ago) show advances in retouching delicate edges. A style of "backed" blades were made from large flakes. The edges were then retouched. The chipped edges were much less likely to break when used. Châtelperronian tools include side scrapers as well as end scrapers. Some Châtelperronian tools were made at sites that look like the homes of Neanderthals, not *Homo sapiens*. Scientists are looking for more evidence there.

Gravettian tools date from 29,000 to 22,000 years ago. During this time, knappers made flechettes for projectile points. These short, leaf-shaped points were retouched at one or both ends.

The Solutrean period was from about twenty-two thousand to seventeen thousand years ago. During this time, projectile points were made in a distinct long oval shape, like a willow leaf. These points were double edged. The base was sharp where the point fitted into a shaft. Beautiful stone would be worked by experts. The result was decorative as well as useful.

The Magdalenian period lasted from about 17,000 to 11,600 years ago. Most sites had exceptionally well made points and burins during this time, as well as saw-toothed knife blades. There is evidence of a long-distance trading network for flint and finished goods.

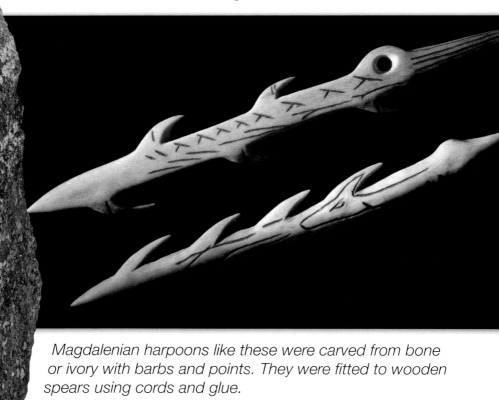

Magdalenian harpoons like these were carved from bone or ivory with barbs and points. They were fitted to wooden spears using cords and glue.

In much of China, the sequence of tools is different from in Europe and western Asia. As bamboo was available, simpler stone tools were useful enough to make many different objects and tools from bamboo. Pottery was also used in China 20,000 years ago, long before the Neolithic.

MAKING STONE TOOLS

Basic flint knapping was apparently a common skill. Many people would have known a little about how to make a basic tool. Most of the better tools and all of the finest ones would have been made by experts. A student would learn by watching and by careful instruction.

Flint knappers carefully prepared and used their materials. Fireplaces show where flint was heated to improve how it would flake. Experts learned to make and repair many types of tools. Blades have been found that had worn dull but were sharpened. Broken points were reshaped. New edges were chipped by pressure flaking.

Worksites were often near but separate from living spaces. No one wants to sleep or cook with sharp splinters underfoot! Knapping is dangerous work. Flint and obsidian break with edges sharper than the surgical scalpels of today. Breathing stone dust causes silicosis in the lungs. Knappers during the Upper Paleolithic would have closed their eyes as they struck. They probably wore leather aprons and hand protectors, but they were still cut by splinters.

COMPOSITE TOOLS

We tend to judge archaeological sites by the stone tools. But these are not the only way to understand how people organized their lives during the Paleolithic Revolution. It's useful to consider how people constructed a composite tool. A stone spear point worked best attached to a wooden shaft with resin glue and bound with cord twined from hemp or nettle. Stone tools were used to prepare a variety of products from organic materials. Several researchers believe organic tools show how the human mind was evolving. Because organic items such as bamboo tools, clothing, or string fibers are rarely preserved, it is still hard to get a full picture of tool making in the Paleolithic Revolution.

CHAPTER 3
ARTIFACTS

Our long-ago hominin ancestors used many other tools besides chipped stones. The artifacts discussed here are tools not chipped from stone and clothes. An artifact (or artefact) is an object or remainder of an object, which was made, adapted, or used by humans. An artifact can be almost anything found at an archaeological site. It can be as big as landscape patterns shaped by human use. It can be tiny trace elements clinging to a broken tool.

CULTURAL INVENTIONS

Sharp stones, sticks, and shells can be found just lying on the ground. Cultural inventions are made because a person thought about what he or she wanted to do. How to carry food except in your stomach? How to hold more than one knife? Among the earliest inventions must have been containers to hold things that people gathered.

Scholar Elizabeth Fisher called this idea the Carrier Bag theory. Some kind of sling or net would be a useful way to carry a baby. A net could be used for other things, too, like catching fish or birds. During the Paleolithic Revolution, people were making useful things from a variety of materials.

People made many useful things from natural materials. Only a few of these artifacts have been preserved for us to find.

Baskets and leather bags decay and leave nothing behind. Wooden house posts or tent poles decay, too. But the holes they leave behind show where the ground was disturbed. Rarely, the wooden handle of a tool will leave a space in the ground that can be filled with plaster. At least the shape of that lost tool can be known.

Stains on many artifacts have been made by red ocher. It has also been found at burial sites. Red ocher has been mined in Australia at the Wilgie Mia mine for at least thirty thousand years. This site is the longest continuous mining operation in the world.

BEADS

It's easy to make simple beads out of animal backbones. People also bored holes through seashells or predator teeth. In the Paleolithic Revolution, people

CARBON DATING

When archaeologists study a cave where people lived during the Upper Paleolithic, there are often tools and bones found in and around cooking fires. Charcoal can be dated using carbon-14 analysis. Carbon dating is a reliable way to date organic artifacts.

This method is based on the rate of decay of natural radioactive carbon 14 atoms found in living matter such as bones. Because carbon 14 decays to a non-radioactive form over time, older samples give off less radiation. The technique estimates an artifact's age by sampling the amount of radioactive carbon left over from when it was formed.

Carbon 14's half-life is 5,730 years. That's how long it takes half of the carbon 14 to decay into nitrogen 14. Samples older than about 30,000 years have only 3 percent of their original carbon 14. By "ultrafiltering" bone samples, researchers can test pure samples. Carbon dating is accurate for items up to 50,000 years old.

made beads from ivory and stone. At some sites, they made far more beads than they'd need for everyone living there to have a necklace.

An Aurignacian site in France's Castelmerle valley was a bead-making factory. Around 37,000 years ago, people

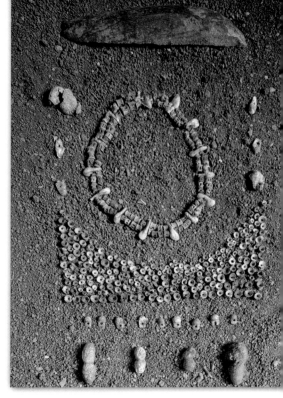

made beads here with mammoth ivory from the Czech Republic. They had soapstone that had been mined from even farther east. The site had separate areas for doing each part of the process to make beads and drill holes. The standard bead was about a quarter inch (6 mm) wide. The result was tens of thousands of beads. Many were woven into clothing. Similar beads have been found as far away as Russia.

Three Paleolithic people were buried at Balzi Rossi, in Italy, with these ivory ornaments and flint knives in their grave.

HUNTING TOOLS

Archaeology used to focus on projectile points because they could be found after forty thpusand years. Wooden shafts rotted away. There were other hunting tools made from wood, which have not lasted. In Australia, people have been using wooden throwing sticks and boomerangs since Paleolithic times.

Harpoons were made with heads that could come off the shaft. Ivory was a good material as it could be carved with barbs along one side or both sides of a

This drawing shows a man using an atlatl during a mammoth hunt. Atlatls continued to be used in North America until the 1500s.

harpoon point. Parts of fishhooks were carved from ivory.

There are many spear straighteners made from antlers with a hole bored through the hardest part. Antler was also carved to make a throwing tool or handle called an atlatl. These handles made it possible to throw small spears called darts or javelins. The atlatl had a small hook at the end that fitted into the butt of the dart. Some atlatls were decorated with engravings or carving. One particularly popular design from a Magdalenian site at Mas d'Azil in Spain had a carved deer. Several similar carvings were found, some with small differences in the shape. There must have been a story behind this carving.

WORKING WITH CLAY

It is frustrating to carve away wood or antler only to find the shape doesn't work well. The carver has to start again with a new piece and try carving another shape. Working with clay instead lets a person add material as well as carve it away. Works in clay are called pottery, whether or not a person makes cooking pots.

Clay can be shaped and decorated in an infinite number of ways. Styles of pottery are much more sensitive to change over time or cultural differences among makers than antler, ivory, or stone. Pottery found from Paleolithic times is almost always broken, but the pieces will last for tens of thousands of years.

At a site in Dolní Věstonice, in the Czech Republic, thousands of pottery pieces have been found. This was an Aurignacian community twenty-eight thousand years ago. One hut had five hearths for firing clay. Another had one hearth in the center. Most of the pottery pieces are animal figures, but there are many human figures as well.

Clay shows impressions. When hardened by fire, the marks remain visible. It's exciting to see the fingerprints

This ceramic bear figurine was found at the Dolní Věstonice site in the Czech Republic.

made by people who shaped clay figures. It's even more exciting to see marks left in clay by twisted rope and cords. The fibers are long-gone but the shape remains.

Some clay shows impressions of basket weaving. This could be accidental from resting a basket on a damp clay floor. It could also be from lining baskets with clay to be waterproof. At Dolní Věstonice, there is a site where huts may have burned down to the clay floor. There are impressions of woven cloth in the hardened clay. These could have been made by cloth bags of clay. Some marks show where people had knelt.

CLOTHING

It's challenging to make definite statements about clothes from the Paleolithic Revolution because there are few remains to prove their existence. The oldest clothing found by archaeologists isn't even ten thousand years old. "Clothes are pretty delicate things and will be preserved intact extremely rarely," said archaeologist Rebecca Wragg Sykes to *National Geographic.* "You can look for other evidence of their presence during more ancient times."

There are tool clues suggesting that Neanderthals and modern humans wore more for clothing than tattered raw animal skins. Microscopic wear patterns on their tools show the work done to prepare clothing. Stone scrapers for working hides became more common during the Ice Ages, when the climate in Europe and Asia was cold. On some stone tools there are organic scraps with tannin from oak trees. Tannin is used to tan leather. Tanned leather can be worked until it was soft enough to be sewn into comfortable clothing. Leather from chamois or ibex was particularly soft. Leather could also be used to make slings for throwing stones.

In some burial sites, there are beads tracing out the outlines of the clothing they must have been sewn onto. Two children were found like this in a twenty-eight thousand-year-old grave in Sungir, Russia. The ground in burial sites is often stained from ocher on the clothes or sprinkled over the body.

SPUN FIBERS

Plant fibers have been found at another site in the Caucasus region from thirty-six thousand years ago. The fibers

People have made fibers from flax plants since the Paleolithic Revolution.

LICE

Another piece of evidence for clothing not being a new invention is lice. Lice that live on human bodies have adapted along with our ancestors. A 2011 study of lice that live on clothing found they have a genetic trail going back to between 83,000 and 170,000 years ago.

were twisted and spun into thread. Some fibers were dyed pink, black, and blue. The plants were flax, which is used to make linen cloth. Bone needles between twenty thousand and thirty thousand years old are delicate enough to sew cloth or make jewelry. At other sites, hemp fibers have been found.

Spinning fibers into thread or string can be done by rolling it on the thigh. But it's faster to use a spindle. Spindle whorls cut from shoulder blade bones have been found at many Magdalenian sites. Only recently have researchers worked with fiber artists to recognize tools used for spinning and weaving. Woven cloth was probably used since the Paleolithic Revolution.

Small statues of women made from clay, stone, or ivory, called Venus figures, date to the Upper Paleolithic. Some of these figures are shown wearing hats, woven belts, and string skirts. Similar string skirts are traditional peasant wear in eastern Europe today. String skirts are also found in Chile on mummies from nine thousand years ago.

Just how much time did people spend making cords and clothing? One kind of evidence is in the bones of the people who lived at the beginning of the Upper Paleolithic. In general, women then were more slender than men. They had different activities from childhood through adulthood. Perhaps part of the work these women did was to spend hours making leather and fibers into clothing and tools. That could explain why their muscles and bones were less sturdy than someone who did more heavy lifting, running, and fighting.

During the Upper Paleolithic era, people wouldn't all have dressed alike. Some would wear ornaments. Children might be dressed more simply than adults. The idea of clothing not just to keep warm in winter but as a thing we choose to wear is as old as the Paleolithic Revolution. People wore clothing not only because the weather was cold. People chose and decorated their clothes.

CHAPTER 4
WORDS

No one knows for sure when humans began to speak. Guesses can be made based on our nearest living relatives: orangutans, gorillas, chimpanzees, and bonobos. All these great apes use some screeches and sounds to show emotions. Some archaeologists think *Homo erectus* was able to speak a few simple words. They had a speech center in their brains. But they didn't have big enough nerves to control their tongues and breath. It's hard to be sure exactly when humans began to speak fluently.

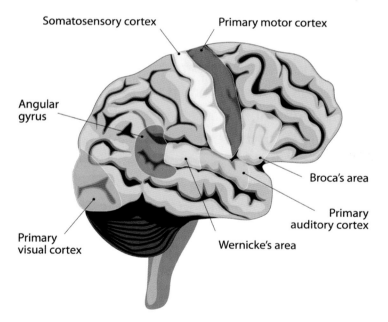

This diagram of a human brain shows areas that are important for communication, which are much larger in modern humans than in our ancient ancestors.

The study of sign language is not as well developed as that of spoken language. Gestures and nonverbal communication are used around the world today. People have invented sign language many times in many places. Our hominin ancestors could have used gestures as well as simple speech to communicate.

SPEECH AMONG MODERN HUMANS

By the time of the Paleolithic Revolution, modern humans were able to say more than a few simple words. They had mouth and breath control for fluent speech and singing. They had dexterity, or good control of their hands, which could be used for gestures and sign language.

As well, their brains had functions that made them able to organize their words with grammar. Neurologists who study brain structure are looking at genes that control brain development. These scientists are learning how brain functions for movement and planning improved our ability to speak and cooperate. When modern humans began making complex tools, they needed to use complex speech for teaching and learning these skills.

ORIGINS OF MODERN LANGUAGE

What language did people speak during the time of the Paleolithic Revolution? Few linguists will discuss the

NEANDERTHAL LANGUAGE

There is indirect evidence for Neanderthals being able to use language. Their bones show that they had speech abilities like those of modern humans. Their tools indicate modern behavior such as making symbols and ornaments. Their minds were probably capable of communicating in symbols.

Another piece of evidence is in their genes. They shared some of the genes relevant to language abilities found in modern humans. And they had children with modern humans. It's very likely that Neanderthals had at least some language abilities, if not a fluent language like we speak today.

subject. It's hard enough to study proto-Indo-European, a language spoken ten thousand years ago that led to the languages spoken in Europe and northern India today. It's harder to see links between that language and proto-Afro-Asiatic. How could a language from forty thousand or fifty thousand years ago be studied at all?

Many linguists feel it is impossible to trace elements of a language so far into the past. After fifty thousand years, wouldn't every word have been changed or replaced many times? Some linguists suggest that we can find the ancient roots of words by comparing hundreds of languages around the world. Perhaps the sounds and structures of old languages could be reconstructed. Linguist Morris Swadesh made lists of basic vocabulary to compare. It is possible that some words in modern Indo-European languages have Paleolithic roots. Linguists think that people in northern Europe may have classified prickly plants separate from fiber plants that were good

to make twine and cloth.

In the past, linguists wondered if language had been invented independently in several places. In recent years, there is evidence that nearly all languages today have their origin in a single place. It seems language began among modern humans living in southern Africa, before their migration to other parts of the world. Scientists Murray Gell-Mann and Merritt Ruhlen believe this language had a grammar rule of subject first, then object, then the verb. A statement like "the man killed a bear" would be said "the man a bear killed."

Today's language groups emerged as people moved farther from Africa. Groups became isolated, and words changed. Modern humans with fluent speech would have had advantages over other people. Language may partly explain why *Homo sapiens* is the only surviving hominin.

One of the basic vocabulary words on Morris Swadesh's list is "horn." Paleolithic people were certainly aware of horns, as you can see in this Paleolithic painting of an aurochs.

CHAPTER 5

ART

A t the time of the Paleolithic Revolution, art became far more sophisticated. People engraved designs on some of their tools. They also made artworks that were not useful tools. There were many pieces of portable art at living sites throughout Europe and Asia. There were also works of parietal art, or rock art that was drawn, engraved, or painted on the walls of caves. It's possible that there were many more works of rock art out in the open that have not lasted.

PORTABLE ART

People made and wore necklaces of ivory or stone beads. Other necklaces were made from predators' teeth and small animal backbones. Small carvings with a hole were worn as pendants.

There were many small pieces of art carved from stone. Sometimes, an image was scratched or engraved onto a flat stone. Some pieces were carved from bone or ivory. Other pieces were shaped in clay. There could be geometric patterns of lines, triangles, or dots.

Small artwork was often made in animal shapes. A common animal such as a bison or horse might be shown. Water animals like otters or seals are rare.

This carving of a bison licking its side was made from a reindeer antler. It was found in the La Madeleine cave in France.

Sometimes, part of an animal would suggest the entire shape. Some horse images look like they might be wearing bridles.

Most interesting are the anthropo-morphs. These figures look part animal and part human. Researchers guess these figures might show shamans or someone having a vision.

HUMAN FIGURES

The portable artworks most studied today are human figures. Some were carved in stone or ivory, others were shaped in clay. Most of the human figures that have been found are female. Most of these figures are not like today's portraits of people with realistic faces. Researchers call these Venus figures, as they might be images of a goddess.

Venus figures are often described as looking dis-torted. Many of these figures look like women with big breasts, bellies, and buttocks. The arms and legs are minimal. The face is not always detailed. Perhaps pregnant figures were holy symbols of the mystery of life.

Other researchers ask a different question. Could the artists have been women, carving figures that looked to them like their own bodies? What looks like obesity could be the way a woman sees her own body when she looks down. The distortion would be realism. The artist would be showing perspective. Perhaps many of the figures were self-portraits made at important times of a woman's life. There are figures of girls, women, pregnant women, and old women.

Some Venus figures were different. At Magdalenian sites near Mezin, in Ukraine, ivory was carved into shapes that look like birds. Look at the fifteen-thousand-year-old figures from a different angle, and they look like plump women.

The Venus of Willendorf was made of limestone rubbed with red ochre. It was found at an Aurignacian site.

CAVE ART

When cave paintings at Altamira in Spain were discovered in 1879, anthropologists were at first unwilling to believe that they were ancient. The paintings were denounced as modern fakes. Anthropologists were reluctant to consider the striking artwork to be more than a few thousand years old.

In 1940, cave paintings were discovered by accident at Lascaux, in France, when four teenagers followed a dog into the narrow entrance of a cave. The hunt was on. About once a year, in Europe and around the world, new sites of cave art are discovered.

Not all caves were suitable for living or for making art. The painted caves have some flattish surfaces like walls that may have been attractive in that time before large buildings. Rock art in caves usually did not decorate living space. In some caves, people lived near the entrance, where sunlight could reach. Art was painted in chambers farther in that were dark and hard to access. Sometimes, a cave where people lived was near a cave that was used for rock art.

Fire made flickering light inside caves. Lamps were just a shallow dish of clay or a piece of rock. Lumps of fat would melt there as a wick burned. If the artist made a handle for the lamp, the wick left burn marks on the side away from the handle. In some caves there are a few smuts from torches made with resin.

GAINING PERSPECTIVE

Scholars had come to think that Paleolithic art had advanced in slow stages from primitive scratchings to skilled work. Then, in 1994, Chauvet cave was discovered in southern France. Carbon dating showed that this great art was approximately twice as old as art in more famous caves. Chauvet's images were art made at the height of the Paleolithic Revolution. Modern humans mastered engraving and drawing at Chauvet cave thirty-five thousand years ago, just a few thousand years after they had come to Europe.

Chauvet cave is an Aurignacian site. In this region's caves, black pigment was made from charred bone or wood. Some of the wood was burned in hearths right inside the cave.

Very few scientists visit this striking art in Chauvet cave. Human breath encourages mold that would damage the paintings, as has happened in Lascaux and Altamira caves.

While most cave art depicts animals that would be hunted for food, at Chauvet the artists drew mostly predators and rhinoceroses. These walls have panels decorated with engravings and drawings. A few are simple outlines. Several show the confidence of a master artist, who can show perspective. Groups of animals show relative distance and suggest movement. Shading is used. One animal is indicated with a series of red dots in a pointillist style like that used by nineteenth-century French artist Georges Seurat.

THREE DIMENSIONS

A cave is not a building with flat walls and ceiling. Upper Paleolithic artists used the texture of rough walls when making their images. At Chauvet, artists drew on bulges and hollows in stone to give their animals realistic curves. Cracks in a wall became the horns of an ibex. These were not flat images.

A similar technique was used in Pech Merle cave, a Gravettian site. Here, a striking mural shows two horses painted on a nearly vertical wall. The head of one horse is painted around a natural projection of the stone. The effect creates the illusion the horses have appeared out of the natural rock. Both horses have spots of paint applied by spitting or blowing through a tube.

At Pech Merle, the main space is fairly large, though the ground is wildly uneven. The shape of the walls makes echoes sound strange in this cave. The acoustics must have added to the experience for the artists and their audience. Visitors today can see footprints in damp clay of a young person from twenty-five thousand years ago.

LASCAUX TECHNIQUES

At Lascaux cave, virtually all the footprints found were made by adolescents, not large adults or children. Twenty thousand years ago, this cave might have been a place for young people to go through rites of passage.

This Solutrean site has around six thousand animal figures in several galleries. In several scenes, horses are painted first. Then aurochs were painted. Then deer were painted. What did this sequence mean? Perhaps the message was about the changing seasons of the year, or which animals to hunt.

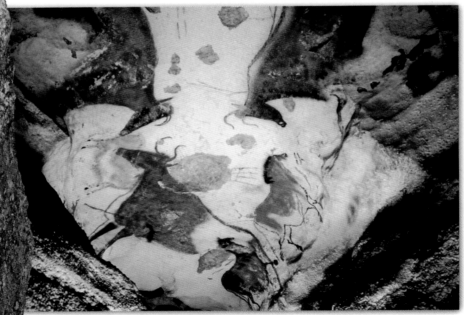

For a hundred years, ancient paintings at Lascaux have been enjoyed by many visitors. Replicas of the magnificent rock art are displayed in a gallery near the original cave.

Some parts of the cave are narrow, while others are wide. In one narrow gallery, the ceiling is high. Artists built scaffolding to make the paintings near that cave's ceiling. The sockets for scaffolding have been found.

In this region, the black pigment is a mineral, manganese dioxide. Painting here was done with brushes and by spraying paint through a hollow bone. The artists showed perspective in several ways. An aurochs near the ceiling was stretched out, so that it would look normal to someone standing below.

HUMAN FIGURES

When humans are shown in rock art, the images are incomplete or unnatural. Usually just handprints are shown. Perhaps a head is drawn, or a penis or vulva shape. There are human figures engraved in the Magdalenian caves of Pech Merle and La Madeleine. They look rough and hasty compared to the animal figures.

One of the few human figures in rock art was found at Cosquer cave. This Solutrean site is near Marseilles, France. The entrance was near the seashore 18,500 years ago. Now the entrance is underwater since the sea level rose after the Ice Age ended. At Cosquer, there are handprints as well as animal figures. The one human figure is controversial. There are marks like arrows across his rough shape. Is this a drawing about a man who was killed? No one knows now what story was being told. At Cosquer, many finished drawings and paintings had lines scratched into or

NIAUX CAVE

Niaux cave is a fascinating Magdalenian site for rock art from fifteen thousand to thirteen thousand years ago. Here, artists needed to economize when using pigments that were rare locally. They would grind up talc (a kind of soapstone) and add the powder to make the pigments go farther. This cave appears to have been used only for the art that was created there. Living quarters for the artists were nearby at Vache cave, only 1,640 feet (500 m) across the valley. That cave was better suited for living, with its cave mouth facing southeast to make the most of the sunlight.

across them afterward.

Perhaps artists had cultural reasons for their choices of image. Birds and fish are rare. There are no landscapes, weather, or trees. Only one drawing of a group of huts has ever been found. Were cave decorations art for art's sake? Some scholars believe instead the images were connected to magical rites or trances.

PAINTED CEILINGS

In northern Spain at Altamira, a cave was found with artifacts from two periods. This was a Solutrean site some 18,500 years ago. Many artifacts have been found here from that period. Altamira cave was a Magdalenian site between 16,500 and 14,000 years ago. That was when a spectacular group of paintings was made.

In 1879, Altamira was one of the first European caves discovered with a large set of cave art. The ceilings are painted with striking images of bison. Four colors of pigment are used: black, yellow, brown, and red ocher. Many of the paintings are sprayed using an airbrush technique. At some earlier sites, artists would spit or blow paint through a hollow bone. At Altamira, artists used two hollow bones. One tube was set upright in a bowl of paint. Using the second tube, the artist blew across the top of the first tube. This made a controlled spray of paint.

When Pablo Picasso was shown the Altamira paintings, he was humbled as a modern artist. "After Altamira, all is decadence," he told his guide.

CLAY WORK

There is an interesting site at a French cave called Le Tuc d'Audoubert. The cave is connected to two other caves under the Pyrenees, a range of mountains in France and Spain. This cave is a Magdalenian site, dating back 13,500 years.

Here, there are many engravings and abstract signs on the walls. Over 385 images have been counted, including paintings and sculptures. In the farthest part of the cave are the most striking works. On a raised pedestal are displayed two clay figures of bison, a female and male. The clay is unfired, still damp. The artist's slim finger marks and tool marks can still be seen. There are other bison marked in clay on the floor. Nearby, a lump of clay shows marks from a child's little hand.

WHO MADE THIS ART?

There are no names on the corner of rock art from the Upper Paleolithic era. Sculptures do not have a maker's mark on the bottom. Perhaps artists showed their ownership of art in different ways. Handprints in many caves might be a sign of ownership. Or they might be a warning to others.

There are some clues to show us a little about who made these artworks. Because many cave paintings show animals, some researchers assumed the artists were male hunters. But sometimes an artist shaping clay had small hands like a woman or a boy.

At Chauvet, there is an animal shape made of palm prints made in red ocher. The maker stood about 5 feet, 10 inches (1.8 m) tall and had a crooked little finger. Other handprints have been measured at eight caves in France and Spain. Based on finger lengths, three out of four handprints were likely made by women.

Sometimes, there are finger marks made in soft surfaces near a painted or engraved figure. These "macaroni" marks might be doodled by an admirer. A few look like a child used his or her small fingers to poke or scribble. Some portable art has engravings with many scratches almost hiding a figure. They might be a kind of meditation.

In this art was the beginning of science, as the artists closely observed nature. They learned the beginning of chemistry as they made paint and glue. This art also shows the beginning of narrative. Stories were being told with these images. Musical instruments and voices echoed in these caves. On the same cave walls as the paintings were marks that were the beginning of writing. Long before recorded history, religion and mythology began with the artists of the Paleolithic Revolution.

TIMELINE

c. 2.8–1.5 million years ago *Homo habilis* lives in East Africa.

c. 2.5–2 million years ago The Paleolithic begins.

c. 1.9 million–70,000 years ago *Homo erectus* lives in Africa, Asia, and Europe.

c. 700,000–200,000 years ago *Homo heidelbergensis* lives in Africa, Asia, and Europe.

c. 400,000–30,000 years ago Neanderthals live in Europe and Asia.

c. 200,000 years ago *Homo sapiens* evolves.

c. 100,000 years ago The first migration of modern humans out of Africa likely happens.

c. 60,000 years ago The second migration of modern humans out of Africa likely happens.

c. 41,000–33,000 years ago Châtelperronian culture exists.

c. 38,000–32,000 years ago Aurignacian culture exists.

c. 35,000 years ago Artists make cave paintings at Chauvet cave.

c. 35,000 years ago The art at Lascaux cave is made.

c. 29,000–22,000 years ago Gravettian culture exists.

c. 28,000 years ago The earliest pottery at the Dolní Věstonice site is made.

c. 25,000 years ago The cave paintings at Pech Merle are made.

c. 22,000–17,000 years ago Solutrean culture exists.

c. 18,600 years ago The paintings at Cosquer cave are made.

c. 17,000–11,600 years ago Magdalenian culture exists.

c. 16,500–14,000 years ago Artists make rock paintings in Altamira cave.

GLOSSARY

acoustics The qualities of a room that affect how sound carries.

anthropologist A person who studies human beings.

archaeologist A scientist who learns about the past by studying the remains and artifacts of past peoples.

atlatl A throwing stick or handle to throw a dart or small spear.

burin A blade with sharp sides and a blunt end.

chamois A wild goat or antelope found in the mountains of Europe.

chisel A blade with dull sides and a sharp, square end.

composite Made of multiple parts.

flax A plant that grows with long fibrous stems.

flint A sedimentary rock formed when minerals dissolved by water are deposited again.

genus A group of closely related living things.

hearth An area that has been prepared for lighting a fire for warmth or cooking.

hemp A plant with long fibrous stems, related to marijuana.

hominin A member of a group of species that includes humans and their ancestors.

ibex A wild goat with long, ridged horns and a beard.

ocher A crumbly mineral of clay stained with iron ore or metal oxides, usually red, orange, or yellow.

prismatic A flaked stone tool with a sharp edge, often triangular or trapezoidal in cross-section.

projectile points Stone or bone points made for spears and darts that can be thrown.

resin The sap of trees, particularly pine and balsam spruce.

rite of passage A cultural experience for a young person becoming an adult.

species A particular type of living thing. Human beings are the species *Homo sapiens*.

For More Information

The Field Museum
1400 S. Lake Shore Drive
Chicago, IL 60605
(312) 922-9410
Website: https://www.fieldmuseum.org
This natural history museum has an extensive collection of
Paleolithic and Neolithic objects, many of them thanks to the
excavations of anthropologist and archaeologist Henry Field.

Flint Ridge Ancient Quarries & Nature Preserve
15300 Flint Ridge Road
Glenford, OH 43739
(800) 283-8707
Website: http://www.flintridgeohio.org
Flint Ridge is a deposit of flint in Ohio, used as a quarry for more
than 10,000 years by Native Americans. Pits where they quar-
ried the flint are still visible on the quarry trail, and inside the
museum an excavated pit is on display. The museum hosts at
least one weekend a year where flint knapping is taught and tool
making is practiced by visitors.

Institute of Human Origins
Arizona State University
PO Box 874101
Tempe, AZ 85287
(480) 727-6580
Website: https://iho.asu.edu
The IHO is one of the leading centers in the world for the study of
human origins. This research center works to bridge social sci-
ence, earth science, and life science approaches. The
IHO fosters public awareness of human origins through

innovative outreach programs. Its materials are useful for both education and the general public. The IHO also maintains a website called "Becoming Human," with considerable learning resources on human origins.

MorphoSource
Contact: Doug Boyer
Trinity College of Arts and Sciences
Duke University
Box 90046
Durham, NC 27708
Website: http://morphosource.org
MorphoSource is a project-based data archive where researchers store and organize, share, and distribute their own 3D images of hominin fossil bones. Anyone can register and download 3D images to use in their own studies.

National Museum of Natural History
10th Street & Constitution Avenue NW
Washington, DC 20560
(202) 633-2950
Website: http://humanorigins.si.edu
The Smithsonian's National Museum of Natural History is committed to expanding the public understanding of human evolution. Its exhibit and website are accessible and informative about the past and the latest research on human origins. The website has a great deal of multimedia materials and teaching resources.

Writing-on-Stone Provincial Park
Box 297
Milk River, AB T0K 1M0
Canada
(403) 647-2364

Website: http://www.albertaparks.ca/writing-on-stone.aspx
Writing-on-Stone Provincial Park is near the town of Milk River in
southern Alberta. It is also known as Áísínai'pi National Historic
Site of Canada. It has been designated a World Heritage Site.
This park serves as both a nature preserve and protection for
a large number of aboriginal rock carvings and paintings. First
Nations people have been living here for over 10,000 years.

Yukon Beringia Interpretive Centre
Box 2703
Whitehorse, YT Y1A 2C6
Canada
 (867) 667-8855
Website: http://www.beringia.com
This center focuses on the journey into the Americas by
Paleolithic people. This museum provides interpretive tours
of its dioramas, films, and exhibits. There are online learning
resources as well.

WEBSITES

Because of the changing nature of Internet links,
Rosen Publishing has developed an online list of
websites related to the subject of this book. This site is
updated regularly. Please use this link to access the list:

http://www.rosenlinks.com/FHEC/paleo

FOR FURTHER READING

Brooks, Philip. *The Story of Prehistoric Peoples*. New York, NY: Rosen Central, 2013.

Currier, Richard L. *Unbound: How Eight Technologies Made Us Human, Transformed Society, and Brought Our World to the Brink*. New York, NY: Arcade Publishing, 2015.

Hatfield, Gary, and Holly Pittman, eds. *Evolution of Mind, Brain and Culture*. Philadelphia, PA: Penn Press, 2013.

Hattstein, Marcus. *Prehistory, First Empires, and the Ancient World: From the Stone Age to 900 CE* (Witness to History: A Visual Chronicle of the World). New York, NY: Rosen Classroom, 2012.

Herzog, Werner. *Cave of Forgotten Dreams*. New York, NY: IFC Films, 2010.

Hurdman, Charlotte. *The Stone Age* (Hands-on History!). Durham, NC: Armadillo Books, 2014.

Meltzer, David. *The Great Paleolithic War: How Science Forged an Understanding of America's Ice Age Past*. Chicago, IL: University of Chicago Press, 2015.

Roberts, Alice. *The Incredible Human Journey*. London, England: Bloomsbury Publishing, 2009.

Stringer, Chris. *Lone Survivors: How We Came to Be the Only Humans on Earth*. New York, NY: Times Books, 2012.

Von Petzinger, Genevieve. *The First Signs: My Quest to Unlock the Mysteries of the World's Oldest Symbols*. New York, NY: Atria Books, 2016.

BIBLIOGRAPHY

Clottes, Jean. "The Paleolithic Cave Art of France." Bradshaw Foundation. Retrieved January 25, 2016 (http://www.bradshawfoundation.com/clottes/index.php).

Drooker, Penelope B. "Approaching Fabrics Through Impressions on Pottery." *Textile Society of America Symposium Proceedings*. Paper 773, 2000. (http://digitalcommons.unl.edu/tsaconf/773).

Garcia-Diaz, M., and M. Vaquero. "Looking at the Camp: Paleolithic Depiction of a Hunter-Gatherer Campsite." PLOS ONE, December 2, 2015 (http://10.1371/journal.pone.0143002).

Gell-Mann, Murray, and Merritt Ruhlen. "The Origin and Evolution of Word Order." *Proceedings of the National Academy of Sciences*. Vol. 108, No. 42, pp. 17290–17295.

Groesbeck, Amy S. et al. "Ancient Clam Gardens Increased Shellfish Production: Adaptive Strategies from the Past Can Inform Food Security Today." PLOS ONE, March 11, 2014 (http://journals.plos.org/plosone/article?id=10.1371/journal.pone.0091235).

Hughes, Virginia. "Were the First Artists Mostly Women?" *National Geographic*. October 9, 2013 (http://news.nationalgeographic.com/news/2013/10/131008-women-handprints-oldest-neolithic-cave-art).

Liesowska, Anna. "First Glimpse Inside the Siberian Cave that Holds the Key to Man's Origins." *The Siberian Times*, July 28, 2015 (http://siberiantimes.com).

Lordkipanidze, David, et al. "A Complete Skull from Dmanisi, Georgia, and the Evolutionary Biology of Early Homo." *Science*, Vol. 342, No. 6156, October 18, 2013, pp. 326–331.

Mayell, Hilary. "Hobbit-like Human Ancestor Found in Asia." National Geographic News. October 27, 2004 (http://news.nationalgeographic.com).

McCall, Grant S. *Before Modern Humans: New Perspectives on the African Stone Age*. Walnut Creek, CA: Left Coast Press, 2014.

Roberts, Alice. *The Incredible Human Journey*. New York, NY: Bloomsbury Publishing, 2010.

Ruff, Christopher B. "Gracilization of the Modern Human Skeleton." *American Scientist*, November-December 2006. (http://www.americanscientist.org/issues/feature/2006/6/gracilization-of-the-modern-human-skeleton).

Sankararaman, Sriram, et al. "The Genomic Landscape of Neanderthal Ancestry in Present-Day Humans." Letter, *Nature*, Vol. 507, No. 7492, January 29, 2014, pp. 354–357.

Sawyer, Susanna, et al. "Nuclear and Mitochondrial DNA Sequences from Two Denisovan Individuals." *Proceedings of the National Academy of Sciences*, Vol. 112, No. 51, pp. 15696–15700.

Soffer, Olga. "Recovering Perishable Technologies Through Use Wear on Tools: Preliminary Evidence for Upper Paleolithic Weaving and Net Making." *Current Anthropology,* Vol. 45, No. 3, June 2004, pp. 407–413.

Stanford, Dennis J., and Bruce A. Bradley. *Across Atlantic Ice: The Origins of America's Clovis Culture*. Oakland, CA: University of California Press, 2012.

Switek, Brian. "Origins of Clothes." *National Geographic*, September 11, 2013 (http://news.nationalgeographic.com).

Thompson, Helen. "Zigzags on a Shell from Java Are the Oldest Human Engravings." *Smithsonian*, December 3, 2014 (http://www.smithsonianmag.com).

INDEX

A

Altamira, cave art in, 44, 51, 52
art, 42–53
      cave, 44–45
      cave ceilings, 51–52
      clay work, 52–53
      human figures in 43–44,
      49–51
      Lascaux techniques,
      48–49
      perspective in, 45–47
      portable, 42–43
      three dimensions in, 47–48

B

bamboo, 25, 26
beads, 28–30, 34, 42
blades, 21–22, 23, 24, 25, 35
bones, 9–10, 12–18
      art made using, 6, 42, 46,
      49, 51–52
      effect of activity on, 12–14
      effect of varied diet on,
      16–17
      needles made with, 35
      of people, 36
      tools made with, 7, 21, 22,
      23, 28
brains, 6, 12, 16, 37, 38
burins, 22, 23, 24

C

carbon dating, 29, 46
carvings, 7, 12, 31–32, 42, 44

Chauvet, cave art in, 45–46, 47, 53
clay, 31–33, 35, 42, 43, 46, 48, 52,
      53
clothing, 6, 12, 26, 27, 30, 33–34,
      35, 38, 40
Cosquer, cave art in, 49, 50

D

Denisovans, 10, 16, 18
DNA, 10, 11, 15, 18

E

engravings, 7, 31, 42, 46, 47, 49,
      52, 53

F

faces, 12, 15
flint, 20–21, 24
      knapping, 20, 23, 25
food, 6, 9, 13, 14, 15, 17, 27, 47

G

genes, human, 6, 12, 17–18, 38
genetic study, 11, 18
genus Homo, 9–10

H

hearths, 32, 46–47
hemp, 26, 35
hominins, 6, 19
      recent, 14–16
      use of speech, 38, 41
Homo erectus, 9, 15, 37
Homo floresiensis, 10, 15

Homo heidelbergensis, 10, 15–16
Homo sapiens, 10, 15, 41

I
ibex, 16, 34, 47
ivory, 7, 8, 23, 28–31, 32, 35, 42, 43, 44

L
language, 38, 39
    origins of modern, 38–41
Lascaux, cave paintings in, 45, 48
leather, 14, 28–29, 34, 38
Lower Paleolithic, 6, 8

M
Middle Paleolithic, 6, 8
    tools of, 22–23

N
Neanderthals, 10, 15, 18, 23, 33

O
obsidian, 20, 21, 25
ocher, 28, 34, 51, 53

P
paintings, 7, 8, 44–45, 49, 50, 51, 52, 53
Pech Merle, cave art in, 47–48
pressure flaking, 21, 25
projectile points, 22, 23, 24, 30

R
resin, 28, 45
rocks
    as tools, 6, 19–20
    used for art, 42, 46, 47, 49, 50, 52

S
spears, 16, 22, 26, 31
speech, 8, 37, 38, 41
    among modern humans, 38
species, 6, 9, 10
    interbreeding among, 17–18

T
teeth, 9, 10, 13–14, 15, 16, 28, 42
tools
    as artifacts, 27, 28
    for hunting, 30–31
    made from flakes, 21–22
    making of stone, 25–26
    Middle Paleolithic, 22–23
    related to clothing, 33, 38
    stone, 6–7, 19–21, 34
    traditions, 22–24
    of Upper Paleolithic, 6, 19

U
Upper Paleolithic, 6, 8, 10, 12–13, 17, 1935, 36, 47, 52

V
Venus figures, 35, 43, 44

W
wood, 7, 22, 26, 28, 30, 31, 46–4

ABOUT THE AUTHOR

Paula Johanson has been a writer, editor, and accredited teacher for thirty years. She has written over two dozen non-fiction books for educational publishers and the novel *Tower in the Crooked Wood*. Her lifelong interest in paleontology takes her on kayak trips through ancient human sites where she has helped scientists gather data on clam gardens and camped on middens that accumulated during thousands of years of use. Her author website is http://paulajohanson .blogspot.ca.

PHOTO CREDITS